T0158823

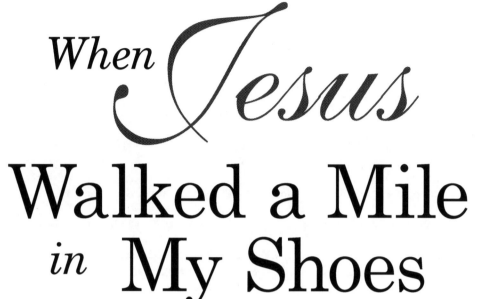

When *Jesus* Walked a Mile *in* My Shoes

CARLOS LEON

WESTBOW
PRESS®
A DIVISION OF THOMAS NELSON
& ZONDERVAN

WestBow Press books may be ordered through booksellers or by contacting:

WestBow Press
A Division of Thomas Nelson & Zondervan
1663 Liberty Drive
Bloomington, IN 47403
www.westbowpress.com
1 (866) 928-1240

ISBN: 978-1-5127-6925-8 (sc)
ISBN: 978-1-5127-6924-1 (e)

Library of Congress Control Number: 2017903389

Print information available on the last page.

WestBow Press rev. date: 3/6/2017

CONTENTS

Ever since I can remember, I always felt that our Lord Jesus Christ and Almighty God both walked alongside me. It is almost as if they walked a mile in the 'shoes of my journey through life". The following is a true recounting of situations and encounters I experienced at various stations in my life. I am sharing these encounters with you in the hopes that you will also share in the love that our Lord Jesus Christ has for each one of us. I also share these encounters to show just how much prayer helped resolve all these difficult situations. I believe my life was saved and serious injuries was prevented by the love of our Lord Jesus Christ and Almighty God. These situations I present to you are not in chronological order. The first chapter is what I believe to be the first incident of Jesus' love intervening on my behalf.

CHAPTER ONE - HEALED BY GOD'S LOVE.

When I was a toddler in Puerto Rico, a serious disease or virus attacked our town. This disease was causing the death of children from birth to age four. I was two years old at that time. I became very ill. We had no doctors near us. All we had were women who played the role of nurses or mid-wives. I became so ill that my mother was told that she should prepare for me to die within a week, if not sooner. One of my sisters knew about a holy lady that was always praying to Jesus especially for the dead or the dying. My sister convinced my mother to let her take me to this holy lady to see if she could stop the disease process and save my life. My mother, having no other recourse, and not having any means of saving my life, agreed to send me to the Holy lady.

The lady informed my mother that she would have to take me way up into the mountains and that I might be gone for several months. Still, my mother agreed and I was taken away from home to be with the Holy lady

From what I understand, the lady offered my illness to Jesus. She stated that if it was Jesus' will, and if my family prayed very hard for Jesus' intervention, Jesus would make the decision to spare my life. It took two weeks before I was completely healed. From what my mother and my sister told me, over 500 children had died in my town and that many of the children who survived had suffered permanent disfigurement on their faces and bodies. I, however, recovered with no ill effects. The word in my town was that I was saved by the love of Jesus and his intervention. I believe what happened is true and in the later years when I visited Puerto Rico, people stilled remembered me as the boy who was spared by Jesus' Love.

CHAPTER TWO - MY CHILDHOOD
"LAST SUPPER" WITH JESUS.

By the time I was six years old, I was already familiar with Jesus and the last supper. It was my understanding that Jesus, knowing he would soon die, asked his Disciples to have a last supper with him. As a child, I understood that Jesus broke bread and passed it around. He also passed some wine around, saying that this represented both his body and blood that He would soon shed for them. I didn't quite understand what Jesus was saying, but I knew that everyone in the church believed his actions were holy and that Jesus meant for this tradition of sharing bread and wine in his honor to be continued.

On the wall above my bed, in the room I shared with two of my older brothers, I had a beautiful picture of Jesus. His image in this picture gave off a great light. The picture was very colorful and Jesus was smiling. I felt every night when I went to sleep, that Jesus would be smiling at me. Under Jesus' picture was a holding cup being held with a nail that stuck out about 1 inch. The cup was used to hold Holy water, but at this time it was dry. So, I decided that I should also offer Jesus some bread and wine. I went to the kitchen and got a large piece of bread. I then place some wine that our Jewish neighbors gave to my mother into the dry empty cup. I wet the bread in the wine and then I placed the moist bread on the nail that held up the cuplike device. I then prayed to Jesus to accept my offer and to bless my house, my family, and to never leave me.

I never moistened the bread again as I had no more wine. Yet, month after month, and year after year, the bread did not spoil or flake off. The bread and the wine remained as moist as when I first placed them to honor Jesus. I didn't think anything about it until I was much older and realized that Jesus had accepted my offer. We lived in that house on Trinity Ave in the Bronx, NYC for several years after

I offered the bread and wine to Jesus. The bread remained moist until we took the picture down because the city bought our house to build a school.

I don't remember what happened to Jesus picture after I moved out of NYC, but I will never forget the smile on Jesus' face. I now realize, being a grown man, that Jesus' love had protected and saved my family and myself, from the dangers of gang warfare and drug issues, that was running rampant in my neighborhood in NYC., N.Y.

CHAPTER THREE - LIGHT CONQUERS DARKNESS.

As a boy of 10, I was familiar with Jesus and I knew that for me to reach heaven, I must pray, stay away from evil and not commit sins. At this age, I was fearful of demons and creatures from hell. I could sense them attacking me at night or when I was alone. I did not know what to do to conquer my fears, so I prayed that the angels would not allow the demons or creatures from the darkness of hell to hurt me.

The day after my prayer, I was waiting patiently for the street light to change so I could cross the street. Without a sound that I could hear, a tall man dressed in dark clothes appeared and stood next to me. Of course I was extremely scared. The man spoke in a very soft and gentle voice and said; "Carlos, close your eyes and imagine that you are in the darkest place you can imagine". Being scared and not knowing how the man knew my name, I closed my eyes and I imagined that I was in a coal mine 500 feet below the ground. It was very dark there. No lights, just darkness. The man said "Are you there yet?" I replied "yes". The man said:" good, now I want you to turn on any light you wish". So not knowing what to light, in my mind I lit a match. The man said "did you turn on a light?". Again I responded "yes". He said "good, now tell me what happened to the dark when you turned on the light". I said "the dark went away where the light was shining". He said "Carlos, I want you to remember this incident always". "As long as you have and keep the light of God and Jesus lit in our heart and Soul, no creatures from the dark or creatures from hell can ever harm you". When I looked up to thank the man and to see what he looked like, the man was no longer standing next to me and had gone away. Now at the age of 71, I think of that moment and I still carry the light of Lord Jesus and God well lit and close to me.

CHAPTER FOUR - JESUS LOVES" LEFT HANDED BOYS" TOO!.

During grade school, I always experienced a difficult time in the classrooms because I was left handed and all the desks were made for right handed students. I was often accused of cheating on the tests because I had to sit sideways so I could write. Unfortunately, it looked to the teachers that I was looking into the other students papers. Most of the time I was reprimanded and sent to the back of the class to take my tests. While sitting in the back of the room, I always managed to get a grade of "A" on all my test, but none of the teachers would take back what they said about me being a cheater. I once tried to tell a teacher that I was not cheating, but because I am left handed, and the desk are made for right handed students, I had to twist and turn my body so that I could write. Needless to say, that was the beginning of a painful storm for me, I was immediately told that I would never go to heaven because Jesus sat on the right hand of God, not His left. My lefthander, to her and to most of my teachers, made me one of Satan's demons .I was devastated. I found that many people in my neighborhood felt that way. I loved Jesus and I loved God, but now I was never going to see them in heaven. This was devastating and my morale was destroyed. I prayed and asked Jesus why couldn't I go to heaven? I was a good boy and did not do anything against God or heaven. I didn't know the meaning of depression at that age, but I believe I was depressed. I tried unsuccessfully to do things with my right hand. Changing to a right handed person was not an option for me. I felt like I was doomed to go to Hell.

One day while playing handball by myself, a man called me over and said he wanted to tell me something important. I was nervous because I did not speak to strangers. Since I saw that many kids were playing near or around me, I moved closer to the man to hear what he had to say to me. He came right to the point of my unhappiness. He said "Do you believe that God makes mistakes?". I replied "of course not, he is God!". Then he asked, "Do you believe that God created you in his image?". I said "yes I do". He said "then you know that God created you left handed because he wanted you to be left handed.". "God did not make a mistake when he created you left handed, the people who are telling you that you will never go to heaven are wrong and they will have to answer to God for telling lies and hurting you". "God loves you as you are and you will always have a place in God's heaven".

I became so happy that I ran past him and went running home beaming with joy. I knew then that Jesus and God loved "left handed boys". I never let the fact that I was left handed ruin my happiness again.

CHAPTER FIVE - JESUS SAVES A "FATHER AND SON" DAY.

During the Korean War in 1952, I was 7 years old. My father was in the U.S. Army serving as a Medic stationed at the front lines. Being a young boy, I did not really understand what war was or that a soldier at war was not permitted to come home anytime he wished. I was in the 2nd grade and my school was going to have a "father-son day". I asked my mother if I could write to dad to see if he could come to my school, dressed as in his uniform for the father-son day celebration. My mother explained that I could write the letter, but that I should not expect dad to attend because he was at war and could not leave his post. I was determined to get my father to come home for this occasion. So, I wrote my father explaining how important it was to have him visit my school for the father-son day. About 2 weeks later, I get a letter from my father saying that he was very sorry that He could not make it, but one day when I was old enough, I would understand why he could not come to the father-son day. I showed the letter to my mother and we both held each other tightly. Mom knew how important it was for me, but somehow, I realized that "No meant No", and that I would have to go to the father-son day alone.

Because I had no father present, I was seated at the back of the auditorium with 3 other boys whose fathers could not come. We were just waiting for the ceremony to start when a big commotion hit the auditorium. Everyone was looking back towards the entrance. I also looked. To my surprise, there was this big soldier in uniform with plenty of medals and stripes. I could not believe my eyes. The soldier asked for his son, Carlos Leon, and I was brought up to him. He just held my hand tight as we were escorted to the front of the auditorium. As it turned out, I was the only boy with a soldier for a father and all the boys wanted to talk to my dad. It made me very proud. Later, I asked dad how come he was allowed to come during war time. He said "did you pray to Jesus to have the army give me permission to come to the father-son day? "I said yes, I did, four times." He said, I prayed too.". "I guess Jesus heard both our prayers". My father left the following morning. It seems the army gave him special permission. When my father showed his Commanding Officer my letter, he broke all the rules to get my father home for 3 days. I will never forget the day Jesus, God, and a Commanding Officer, allowed a soldier to leave a war zone just to spend a few hours with his son. Later in life, when I was a soldier, my daughter Bridget asked me to attend a father-daughter day at her high school. I was away on assignment, but the Lord Jesus and myself moved mountains to be there for her as my father was for there for me.

CHAPTER SIX - MY MOTHER VISITS HEAVEN AND CONFIRMS ITS EXISTENCE;

One of my most treasured memories in life occurred when I was overseas and received a Red Cross telegram stating that my presence was requested immediately in NYC. My mother was in critical condition and did not have much time to live. I was granted permission and given 14 days emergency leave so I could attend to my mother. It was an 18 hour flight and during the flight I was frightened that my mother would die before I got there. I prayed to Jesus, to God, and to all the angels in heaven to keep her alive so I could once again and for the last time tell her how much I loved her. A man can pray a lot of prayers in 18 hours, and I did. As an 18 year old sailor, and the tough man I thought I was, I once asked my mother if she would be offended if I did not cry when she died. At that time in my life, I shed very few tears. My mother said that it was ok since she knew how much I loved her. Now on the plane, I could not stop the tears and I wanted to tell my mother that this tough warrior does cry.

When I arrived at the Naval Hospital in Queens, NYC, my mother had suffered her 10th cardiac arrest and the doctors decided that she would not be put through the pain of more chest compressions again. I was too late. TOO LATE. My mother had passed on. My father was in the room when I walked in and he told me Mom had just died. We held each other while the nurses cleaned up my mother, combed her hair, and removed all the tubing that was connected to her. My dad asked me to call my brothers and sisters to notify them that mom had passed away. My dad went to sign autopsy papers in the basement of the hospital while I prepared to make those calls. I had six sisters and 3 brothers to call. It took me a while, at least 45 minutes due to crying with each of them on the phone. I then noticed that my father was exiting the elevator getting ready to enter my mother's room. I got is attention and asked him to wait for me before entering her room.. He did so.

We both entered the room together. My mother looked peaceful and the nurses had done a great job in making her look lovely. My father went to her side at the head of the bed while I placed myself at the foot of the bed where the doctors and nurses kept their notes on a clip board attached to the bed. My father was talking to my mother as if she was alive. I was mentally telling mom that I love her and that I had indeed shed plenty of tears for her and that I was going to miss her deeply. Approximately 5 minutes after entering the room, my mother opened her eyes and smiled at us. We both went into a semi shock. My father, a medic in the army, knew that my mother had died 50 minutes ago. My father immediately pushed the button for the nurse. Meanwhile, my mother started talking. My father told me later that she had not been able to speak for at least 10 days before being placed in the hospital. My mother began to speak and tell us about how a beautiful angel with big lovely wings sat her on a soft cloud and as he opened his wings, my mother said that she was able to see everything that happened from the moment that God had created the Earth until the moment she died. My father asked her if she had seen Jesus or God? My mother said that she did not, but that the angel told her that when she returned back to heaven in a few minutes, she would meet God, Jesus, and all the Saints in heaven.

At that point, she looked at me and asked me to get a paper and a pen. She said she wanted to write a message. So I ripped a nurse's note paper and a pen and gave it to my mother. As she was writing I was telling her how much I loved her and how much I was going to miss her. I told her that I did cry a lot when I felt she would die before I got to see her, but now that she was back with us, I was happy.

The nurses had come in while my father was talking to my mother and they were astonished and confused to see my mother alive. They called for the doctors to come in the room "STAT" which means "immediately". The nurses did not interfere with my father or me and just waited for the doctors to come in.

At this point my mother gave me back the note she had written and smiled at my father. We both were telling her how much we loved her when her eyes closed, This time we knew that she was dead and was on her way to meet God, Jesus, and the Saints as the beautiful angel had told her..

I gave my father the notes my mom had written before she truly died and let him read it out loud. At this point, a couple of doctors had come in the room and started to evaluate my mother. The nurses confirmed that my mother had awakened and had written the note my father was going to read. The note was simple but it said the following: "Please tell my children not to worry or to be sad. I know that I am going to heaven and I have no fear". Please thank the doctors and the nurses for the care that they gave me". I love you". 'Juana". (Juana is my mother's name)

The doctors and nurses all told us that my mother indeed died the first time. No heart beat, no blood pressure, and no brain waves for at least 8 minutes before they had declared her dead. No one had an explanation for what had just occurred. The doctors and nurses left the room leaving my father and me alone with my mother. Dad said that it was God who allowed her to come back to Earth to let us know about heaven and about the love she had for us.

I believe it was my prayers to Jesus and to God that allowed me to see my mother so I could tell her I loved her and that I had indeed cried for her. I was allowed to accomplish this and I will forever be grateful to God and Jesus for allowing me that special time with my Mother. My Father and I shared this event with the family and as painful as it was to lose our mother, the fact that she came back to let us know she was going to heaven helped with the pain and the sorrow. My sister Inez still has the original copy of my mother's note.

CHAPTER SEVEN - CHOKING AND MY PRAYERS TO JESUS:

Like most children, I loved to eat candy. Generally, I chewed the candy and had no problems swallowing it, therefore thoroughly enjoying the candy. This one day, I happened to get a candy that was hard and round like a large marble. I couldn't bite it in half, so I decided to just suck on the candy until it became small enough to break into pieces. I was in the school yard and basically, I was alone as I preferred to be. My house was always full of siblings and their guests, so I truly preferred the peace and quiet of solitude. I really do not know what occurred, but suddenly I found myself chocking on this large piece of round, hard candy,. It completely blocked my airway. I panicked and fell to the ground. I could not breathe and I saw that my fingers were turning blue. As I grasped my neck trying to dislodge the candy, I started to pray to Jesus. Please Lord, do not let me die alone here in the school yard. I just prayed and prayed while I was becoming more and more blue. I felt as if I was going to pass out and die. All of a sudden, I felt like something or someone had pushed my stomach and the ball of candy went flying out of my throat. I was able to breathe again and my blue color went away. I just stood there crying. I saw the candy lying on the floor and with all of my energy, I smashed it with my foot into millions of pieces. I swore never to eat round hard candy. As I walked back to my house, I thanked Jesus 100 times for saving my life. I had no other explanation as to why the candy flew out of my mouth. To me, it had to be the work of Jesus and the Heavens. I told my mother what happened and she said that I was very lucky that Jesus had sent a special Guardian Angel to help me during that difficulty. My mother said the reason why I was saved was because "Jesus heard your prayers and sent a Guardian Angel to help us with your problem". To this day, I do not eat or give my grand children any round, hard candy.

CHAPTER EIGHT - THE 23RD PSALM - HELP FROM ABOVE:

One incident that captured my heart takes place in a hospital setting. I was an Oncology Nurse and most of my duties circled around patients who were about to die imminently. It was a very hard assignment and most nurses did not want to work in such a depressing atmosphere. When I became a nurse, I wanted to serve in the most difficult areas so that I could bring my Lord Jesus Christ and God's love to my patients. Most of whom had little or no hope of surviving terminal cancer. I knew their pain was severe, not just because of their terminal condition, but because they were going to lose everyone and everything they had ever loved. I felt this was where the heavens needed me the most.

On this occasion, a patient who was in the active process of dying, called me to his bedside. I could see he was having difficulty breathing and I did all I could to make him comfortable. He had requested to die without medical interference, so I respected his right to do so. After making him comfortable, he asked me if I could read him the 23rd psalm before he died. I went into a state of panic. I am a Christian, but at that time I didn't know how to find items in the Bible. I did not want to disappoint this dying man and I felt I had very little time before he died, so I could not leave the room for help. I also did not want him to die alone. I held the Bible in my hands and I said to the heavens: "Lord, I do not know how to find the 23rd psalm in the Bible." "This child of God is asking me to read this psalm to him before he dies". "I want him to die in peace hearing the specific words from the 23rd psalm he needs to hear". "Lord, Will you help me please?". I took a deep breath and looked into my patient's eyes, eyes that had faith in me to read the 23rd psalm. I opened the Bible and looked down into the page I opened. I was totally washed in happiness. There before me I had opened the Bible to the 23rd psalm. With tears in my eyes and holding one of my patient's hands, I read the 23rd psalm to him.

When I finished reading the psalm to him, he squeezed my hand tightly and then he thanked me. He continued to hold my hand for another 2 minutes before he died. Afterward, in the room, I could not move. I was transfixed with what had just happened. A hand from heaven must have guided my hand to open the Bible to the exact psalm the patient wanted. To me, it had to be the guiding hand of Jesus in answer to my prayer asking for assistance. Today, I still hold this moment as a sign that Jesus lives in all of us. All we have to do is keep the faith.

CHAPTER NINE - ZIP GUNS AND THE POLICEMAN:

When I was 11 years old, I lived in a section of the Bronx, NYC, that was dominated by gangs. If you didn't join the gangs, you were severely beaten every time they saw you. You either joined them, or in some cases, did jobs for them. The gang members, knowing that my father was a tough soldier, did not beat me up, but

when my father was away, the gang members would scare me into doing things for them. In NYC, at that time, there were policemen who "walked the beat" in their neighborhood. These policemen knew what was going on in their beats, and knew the bad kids from the good kids.

On this occasion, the gang across the street asked me to carry 6 homemade guns called "zip guns". They wanted me to move them away from the police on the beat and bring them to another gang that was waiting for them on the next street over.

This particular policeman was very friendly with my family as he knew that none of us disrespected or created any issues against the law. He also knew when my father was away on military assignment. On this day he saw me walking holding a medium size bag that looked heavy. Knowing me as one of the good boys, he came over to say "hi". When I returned the greeting, he noted that I looked scared and nervous. Looking at me with curious eyes, he asked me what I was carrying in the bag. I was stumped. I knew lying was bad and lying to the police was worse. At this point I began to pray to Jesus to help me because I believed I was going to go to jail. If I got arrested, I would embarrass my mother and when my father returned, I would get punished. I had no recourse but to tell the policeman that I was carrying guns for a gang located on the next street over.

The policeman took the bag from me and looked inside and found the 6 guns I had mentioned. Then he looked at me and said "I know you and you are one of the good kids in the neighborhood" "What are you doing carrying guns for gang who would use these guns to either kill or injure people"? Crying, I told him the story of how the gangs threatened me and my family with bodily harm and death if I didn't work for them. The policeman recognized my fear and smiled at me. He said he would not arrest me or even report me to the police or my family. He said that by telling him the truth, he understood my dilemma and would try to help me. He walked me back to the gang members who gave me the guns and told them that if he ever found out that I was doing jobs for them or if I or any of my family was hurt or otherwise injured, he and the rest of the police would come immediately to arrest them and break up their gang.

The policeman asked me if I believed in Jesus. I said I did. He then told me that if I ever was in any trouble, to ask Jesus for guidance. Also, he told me that just like Jesus, he too was my friend and that I could talk to Jesus or him anytime I wanted. He said that to be a man you have to behave like a man and do the right things. I learned two lessons that day. One, that I was not the only person who had taken Jesus Christ into their hearts, so had the policeman. The second lesson is that a man should always do the right things, even if it is very difficult, even when no one is looking.

CHAPTER TEN - A CHRISTIAN RADIO STATION INTERVIEW:

This next incident occurred while I was going to college for my nursing degree. It was during a lunch break. I was outside under a tree reading out of one of my nursing books. I noticed a group of people coming in my direction. It happened to be the Christian Radio staff that were interviewing students at the college regarding their individual beliefs in Christ. I invited them to sit down and ask any questions they had. During the interview, I was asked if I was a born again Christian. At that time it was a new saying and I had not heard the term until that interview. I tried to qualify my answer as follows: I don't know what you mean by "born again Christian". I think it means that some Christians have departed from the ways of Christ and now have returned to worship Christ. Like many other Christians that I know personally, I have never left Christ and I know deep down in my Soul, that Jesus has never left my side. "Jesus", I said aloud," I am glad that these lost Christians are finding their way back to you". If they want to be called born again Christians, well, more power to them.

They thanked me for my honesty and I continued with my studies.

That evening and for many, many evenings after, I received phone calls from people I did not know thanking me for my prayers and for placing Jesus at the head of the line in my life. Many people who heard the broadcast stated that I touched them with my honest opinion of Jesus Christ and that they would pray for me. I thanked them and I felt an overwhelming warmth that could only come from God's love.

Chapter eleven - Catholic Nuns on a train:

One beautiful sunny Sunday I was riding a train in Southern Spain.

It was a shortly after President Kennedy was assassinated and half dollar coins were circulated in his honor. I happened to purchase thirty of these coins prior to taking my trip through southern Spain. I was stationed in Rota, Spain where my duties required me to repair or replace broken communication equipment on our Nuclear Ballistic Submarines. I was enjoying my trip when the train made a station stop. Twenty-six Catholic nuns boarded the train and entered the compartment I was sitting in.

One of the nuns sat next to me, introducing herself she remarked that she and the other nuns, belonged to a specific religious order. Sadly, I do not recall the order to which they belonged. In our conversations, she found out I was an American sailor, so we started talking about President Kennedy. Nearing the end of the conversation, I mentioned that I had a half-dollar coin with Kennedy's image on it. She asked to see it and I took one out of the bag that I was carrying the Kennedy half dollar coins in and showed it to her. The coins were new and very shinny. She held it in her hands and placed the coin next to her heart. She had a look on her face of adoration and tranquility. Seeing that look upon her face, there was no way I could ask her to return the coin, so I told her that she could keep it. She was so pleased and happy that she jumped up out of her chair and began to show the coin to the other nuns. The coin created a commotions on the train. There was so much excitement, you would have thought that a person had won a billion dollar lottery. Well, the leader of the nuns, a "Mother Superior", came to me very humbled and asked if I had another coin that she could have. She explained that President Kennedy was a catholic and the people of Spain adored him. I was faced with 25 other nuns who wished they too could own a Kennedy coin. Well, I stood up and said that if they would line up, I would give each one of them a Kennedy coin. I will never be able to measure the joy and the happiness expressed by these nun on receiving a Kennedy half-dollar coin. I was hugged by each of them. They each told me that for the rest of their lives, they would pray to Jesus for my safety, my health, and for a safe trip to where I was traveling to on that day. They all said that their prayers would include a quick trip to heaven when my time on Earth was done.

I felt honored that so many dedicated Christians would devote time to pray for me. I believe it was not a coincidence that I purchased 30 Kennedy coins prior to taking that train trip, and then to meet with a group of Catholic nuns on the same train, who would treasure these coins, and in return, Pray to Jesus for my well being. I believe that Jesus had a hand in this incident.

CHAPTER TWELVE - FEAR GRIPS ME AS MY SUBMARINE BEGAN TO SINK.

I know that sometimes in our lives, some of us will experience an incident that will shake us down to our foundation in total fear. I have experienced a few, but this next incident will stick in my mind for the rest of my life. In 1963, I was a submarine sailor in an old World War II diesel submarine. I had been on this sub for nearly nine months and I was still in training for my Submarine Qualification

Dolphin Pin. I think I had been involved with at least 200 submarine dives in deep waters and had no real fear of diving underwater. To get an understanding of balance in a submarine, you have to know that when a submarine is on top of the water, there is no way of knowing in which part of the submarine the ballast water is located . If the ballast water is in the forward part (bow) of the submarine when we dive, the sub will then go bow first and lift the stern (rear or back end) of the sub, out of the water. If the ballast water is towards the stern, when we dive the sub will tend to go stern first and keep the front of the sub pointing up out of the water. If the ballast water is in the middle of the sub, the dive will go smoothly. Each submarine has a crew assigned to keep the ballast water in the center of the sub by pumping water back and forth to what ever part of the submarine the water is needed to have a smooth and successful dive.

Well, on this dive, we had a school of submarine students in the forward torpedo room. We also had a full compliment of war torpedoes in the forward torpedo room. And unfortunately, the ballast water was also located in tanks under the forward torpedo room. My station during a dive was to man the Emergency Communication Buoy. When its lever is pulled, the buoy breaks away from the sub, floats to the surface and sends an SOS signal. The buoy is attached by a wire several thousand feet long. The purpose of this buoy is to notify any rescuers that a dead submarine is attached at the bottom of the wire. At that time, there were no fast ways to get to a sunken submarine, Usually it would take a week or longer for a submarine rescue ship to arrive on scene. We could only manufacture 18 hours of oxygen after the oxygen inside the submarine was used up. This process took approximately sixteen hours, leaving us with less than 2 days of oxygen. It would take a rescue vessel five days to reach us. Each sub sailor knew this was always a possibility but no one wished it to be. There was little chance of escaping if the sub descended more than 150 feet into the depths of the ocean. As we made the dive, I immediately, knew something wasn't right because I was slammed against the forward wall in the radio room. I could hear the captain trying his best to correct the steep angle of our descent. Nothing was working and the sub was pointing straight down. I made my way towards the door of my radio room and opened it. Across from the radio room door is the station where all the air control valves to blow air into the ballast tanks are located. By blowing air into the water filled tanks, the water is forced out of the tanks and the sub becomes lighter and can then float to the surface. I looked at my friend who was stationed there. He had 16 years of submarine experience, and he looked concerned, confused, and fearful. None of his actions or attempts to blow the water out of the tanks had helped the Captain to get the sub to start rising. He looked me in the eyes and said, "Good bye Carlos, It has been nice having you for my friend". With that, I went back into my radio room and shut the door. I began to pray that Jesus would give me the strengths and courage to die with honor.

I knew that we were going to die and that our bodies may never be found if I did not get back to my post. I went to my post and began to pray again. To pray is not exactly the right words, I mean I began to pray with all the emotions that the fear of suffocating under water could bring to my mind.

Still, the sub would not surface. All I could do was pray that I did not fail in my tasks. I knew that there were many new students and crewmembers who I felt they did not deserve to die. If anyone had to die, I asked Jesus to spare them and take those of us who knew what we were getting into. In what seemed like a lifetime of waiting, the submarine finally started to float up and just bounced off the bottom in a flat position. The submarine immediately started rising up quickly because it was now lighter than the water.

We were all saved. The sub could have hit bottom bow first and we would have all died, or moved another 200 yards further, the sub would have sunk in over 1000 feet of water which would have crushed our hull and killed all of us. This sub was not built to go below 600 feet deep without collapsing its hull. Luckily, we had only suffered minor physical injuries when we bounced off the bottom. As to the emotional or mental injuries, I will never know their extent because no one talked about their feelings. I venture to say that I prayed and prayed a lot. The other crewmen also stated they had prayed. I believe that the hand of Jesus was there to help us out. A million things could have gone wrong that day, yet what comes to my mind is that my prayers and the prayers of my fellow crewmen, caused Jesus to intervene on our behalf and save our lives.

CHAPTER THIRTEEN - A MEDICINE MAN'S PRAYERS:

The next two incidents occurred while I went with my son Carlos, to a cowboy ranch. We belonged to the "Indian Guides", a father-son organization similar to the Boys Scouts. We had approximately 15 Indian tribes with approximately 200 young boys. At this cowboy ranch, there were cows and horses. The boys and their family members who accompanied them were enjoying themselves immensely.

I took a group of about 30 boys to see a round-up of cows in the bull-ring area. After the round-up, the boys were allowed into the bull-ring to touch the cows. Without warning, a large bull with sharp horns started charging across the ring towards the boys, which also included my son. I was just one week into recovering from right knee surgery and still had pain and stiffness whenever I waked. Still, I got to my feet and prayed to Jesus to allow me to get the speed and strength to stop that bull before it caused any injury to the boys. I had never tackled a cow or bull before, but I knew that I had to do it. As I started running, I noticed that some of the staff of the ranch were getting to their feet and shouting for someone to stop that bull. I believed Jesus heard my prayer because I ran faster than I ever thought possible. In fact, I ran and was able to get in front of the charging bull. I don't know how I was able to stop and tackle that beast, but before I knew it, I had the bull on the dirt and my arms around its head and horns. A tremendous cloud of dust flew up into the air where the cow hit the ground. The cow got up slowly, confused, and turned and walked away from the boys. The staff, noticing me favoring my right knee, ran up to me to see if I was injured. By a miracle, I was not. I know I that I could have been seriously injured by that charging bull, but heaven saw fit to keep me from harm. The staff thanked me, not only for saving the children, but for saving them from a law suit if any of the children would have been injured. I told them not to thank me, but rather, to thank our Lord Jesus for guiding my speed and action. Afterward, the parents were informed of what had occurred and the actions I took to save their children. I was thanked profusely. In turn, I asked them to thank God. I truly believe that if it wasn't for Jesus' intervention, many of the children would have been injured or killed.

During the same week long camp out at the ranch, the Indian Guides were going to have a big celebration announcing the winners of the many contests we had during the week and to announce the overall camp champion.

The event was scheduled for 3 o'clock in the afternoon. Well, it started to rain and the forecast was for rain all afternoon into the evening. Since this final celebration is an out-door event held in a large open area, the rain was going to spoil the event. Because I was the Medicine man for the Indian Guide Nation and I held the Holy Position of Trust, I was asked to see if I could stop the rain. No one believed it could be done and no one believed that the Medicine man could do anything at all to obstruct mother nature. I decided to pray to the Lord Jesus, inviting the boys to join me in prayer. I think I got about 75 boys to join me in prayer. The Medicine Man prayer session took place from 1:30 p.m. until 2:00 p.m. At 2:45 p.m., the rain stopped and it did not start again until 7 p.m. that night. Many parents were saying that it was just luck that the rain stopped, not our prayers. I calmly asked these parents if they would tell their children that praying to the Lord Jesus to stop the rain, was just a foolish act when only luck was responsible to save the ceremony? None of these parents volunteered to speak to their child. I guess prayer is still precious in their lives. I firmly believe that without our prayers, the rain would not have stopped.

I also believe that the Good Lord's ears are blocked from his children only by a thin layer of love that can be moved aside by our prayers. I believe in my heart that Jesus heard the pleas for sunshine and in his infinite goodness, gave the Indian Guides their sunshine as their prayers requested.

CHAPTER FOURTEEN - " LOVE THY ENEMIES":

The following incident will live with me until the day I die. I was traveling in South Vietnam trying to find my new command who were located somewhere in the most southern part of the Mekong River in Vietnam. My new command had been attacked with armor piercing missiles destroying most of the communication equipment. Many of the ship's crew had been injured. Being a sailor and not assigned to any of the Navy or Army units in the area, I was not issued a weapon. The concern was since I didn't belong to anyone, I did not have to account for the rifle once I returned home from Viet-Nam. Mainly, I depended on the Army units for transportation, protection, food, and for information on where my command was located. I traveled by army trucks, army planes, and army helicopters. My trip was from Saigon to the most southern place in Vietnam. It took me approximately 18 days to get to my new command. During my travels to find my command, I experienced army posts that were under enemy attacks as well as coming under sniper fire. When I was asked to be the truck's shotgun rider I did so. These were events of war and although very scary, I was well protected by the army units. At the far end of South Vietnam, on the Mekong River, I was picked up by a unit of Green Berets who were patrolling the river where my new command was supposed to be located. Since the naval vessel I was trying to find had no communication systems available, It would depend on visual sightings until I could arrive to fix the damage. After repairs, I could help the command leave Viet-Nam for Japan to receive extensive repairs. Finally, I was escorted to a very small landing pier that the navy occasionally used. I was about 50 yards from a village. The Green Beret who escorted me was African American and he told me to be very careful because the Viet-cong had orders to injure or kill minority servicemen so that the they could use the casualties as a propaganda tool, showing that America was sending their minorities to war just so they could be killed or injured and removed from sight in America. Being a Puerto Rican American and tan in skin color, I fit the description of a minority.

The Green Beret soldier also informed me that the village I could see a mere 50 yards away was a known Viet-Cong supported village. They were considered by the Green Beret's to be 90% communist. He informed me that he had radioed for my pick-up but he was not sure how long it would take for the Navy to get to me. He told me he had to go and that at minimum, I should have been issued a rifle for defense. He wished me well and then departed leaving me alone, It was high noon and the sun was bearing down on me like I was the only one left to burn. I was hot, tired, hungry, and scared. I did not dare to move away from that little pier for fear of attracting attention from the enemy. All I had to defend my self was a combat knife. After a few moments, I noticed movement in the village. It seemed that a group of about 15 men were approaching me. Thinking about what that Green Beret had told me, I expected these men to be either Viet-cong or viet-cong sympathizers. Either way, I was going to be killed or captured. Because I had a Top Secret Crypto Clearance, I knew that if I was captured, I would definitely be tortured for the information I possessed. Having completed survival and resistance training, I knew what their torture would be like. I could think of nothing else except that this was going to be my last day on Earth. The closer the men came to me, the more I asked Jesus to help me to be brave in the face of my enemies. If I was to die, I was going to take one or two of them with me. I had marshal arts training and I felt I could at least put up a good fight before I died.

Finally the group of men reached to me. I placed myself with my back to the river so I could face them and not let them get behind me. All at once, the men started talking and pointing to different areas around me. Some pointed to the river, some pointed to the sun, and many pointed to my abdomen area and mouth. I knew only basic Vietnamese, but these men were speaking very fast and I was very scared. They stayed talking to me for about 10 minutes. All the time I was expecting them to attack me. I prayed some more. To my surprise, the men left. I was really concerned. If they had not killed me now, perhaps they thought that I had friends covering my back and left to get more help. I tried listening for the Navy boat, but I couldn't hear anything. I could not move because the Green beret told me this was the only pick-up point for the Navy. I was sure left in a mess. I was upset with the Navy for not providing me with better transportation. Again, I saw commotion at the village. This time a larger group of villagers were coming and bringing or carrying items that I could not see or easily identify.

My fear and concern returned to me. These people went back for reinforcements and were coming in greater numbers to kill me. I was doomed and I knew it. So, again I prayed for courage and to behave like an American fighting man. The man who led the first group started talking and pointing. I was stiff and did not want to make a move that would be conceived as an attack on them. Soon, I had women as well as men set up a giant beach umbrella. Other men pulled me into the shade. I was presented with a basket of fruits and jugs of water and some unknown juice. All I could think was that instead of shooting me or cutting me up into pieces, they were going to poison me. At no time did I realize that these villagers were offering me food, drink, and shade. I finally decided it would be better to eat and die of poisoning than to be tortured to death.

I ate several fruits and drank water and their strange juice. I enjoyed the shade, and I realized that no harm was going to come to me from these people.

I smiled and talked to them in what little Vietnamese that I knew.

They were with me 25 minutes the 2nd time. Soon, the villagers became restless and took down the beach umbrella and started pointing to the mouth of the river. They gathered their food and water and left in a hurry back to their village. I was amazed at what happened. I was fed and provided shelter by people I expected to be my enemies. I thanked God, Jesus, and the heavens for the good fortune that was provided to me. Within a few minutes of the villagers departure, a small Naval boat came up the river to pick me up. The sailors were deeply concerned for my safety and stated that they tried to get here as soon as they could because they had lost some men in this same spot last month. They asked me if the people from the village tried to hurt me and I said no, to the contrary, they were very friendly. The sailors did not believe me in the slightest. While on the Navy boat heading for a stop over station before I reached my command, I prayed again and I asked Jesus to protect those people and give them all the blessings that God could offer. I thanked Jesus again for my life.

CHAPTER FIFTEEN - BLACK ICE:

At the time of this incident, I was living in North Dakota where my wife was working her fist job as a family physician. We wanted to serve in a rural area, and this little town of 1200 qualified as rural. I know that people may not like North Dakota due to the very cold winters, but for a man who loves hot climates, I learned to love it.

The fact was that in our town, the snow usually came by the end of October and stayed until April or May. The summers were short but somehow, the farmers were able to plant and harvest on time. On this particular day, I decided that while my wife was working, I would go to a large city and get some fish that we could not get in our town. Since the back roads generally are safer and less traveled, I took the back roads. The town I was going to shop at was two hours away. It was a clear day but very chilly with a temperature around 10 degrees (F). The snow was off the roads and pushed to the side of the roads. About 20 miles from home, I was driving on a long flat road that looked clear and safe. I was only going about 40 miles per hour and the speed limit was 60. Without any warning, my car started to fish tail and spin around. I was trying hard to control the car, but I knew it was going to be a losing battle. On both sides of the road were steep declines about 40 feet deep at a 30 degree angle and at the end of each decline was a half frozen lake. I noticed that the car was sliding sideways towards the decline on the right side of the road. I knew that if the SUV fell into that decline, I was going to tip over and slide right into the lake. If that happened, I would be wet in 10 degree weather. Being that the road was only lightly traveled at that time of day, it was going to be a very long time before anyone would notice I was in trouble and needed help. All I could do was say a quick prayer. I said "oh no Lord, please don't let me crash into the lake". The car was still moving to the edge of the road and I knew for sure I was going to fall down the steep decline into the lake. As the car started to slide down the decline, I said "Lord, if I have to fall into the lake, will you please stay with me to the end?" I continued to pray while the car was sliding down sideways towards the lake. At any moment the high center of gravity on my car was going to make the car flip on its side. All I could do was hold on for dear life.

Well, the Lord heard my prayers because the car did not tip over! It stopped at the edge of the lake. I think I was still paralyzed with fear, but I knew that the Lord had once again saved me from a very bad situation. Now all I had to do, was figure out how to get out of this large hole I was in. I asked Jesus to be by my side as I tried to get the car and myself out of this situation. I tried twice, sliding back down without flipping over. On the third try, I was able to drive up the steep snow covered embankment, and back onto the roadway. No cars had passed during the time I was in danger. When I got to the roadway, I thanked Jesus for helping me survive that horrific experience. I decided to forget the fish and to just drive back home. Needless to say, I drove the car back home at a speed of 20 miles per hour. I didn't see any cars on the road as I made my way home. I am truly glad that Jesus not only hears our prayers, but answers them as well.

CHAPTER SIXTEEN - MY WAR TIME NURSE WAS AN ANGEL:

The day after I had arrived in Japan from Viet-Nam, I went to surgery to fix my right wrist that had been shattered while in Viet-Nam. It was the fall of 1969 and the Viet-Nam war was still going on strong. The Naval Hospital Yokosuka, Japan was the main hospital to receive the Navy and Marine casualties coming in from Viet-Nam. Most of the hospital's wards housed anywhere from 50 to 80 patients The wards were open and no private rooms were available. The ward that I was in held about 70 patients, mainly young wounded Marines and 3 other sailors. After surgery, my body was racked with severe pain. A deep burning bone pain that would not leave me alone. The pain seemed to dig deep and then deeper into my Soul. The pain was indescribable, and whether I liked it or not, the pain usually brought tears to my eyes. I tried praying for courage and for strength to deal with my pain, but it seemed that the pain would not allow my prayers to reach heaven. Every day several young severely wounded Marines were brought to the Ward. Since I was the only patient at that time who could get out of bed by himself, all the newly wounded Marines were placed on either side of my hospital bed. This way I could call for help if I felt these Marines needed the Nurses, There were only 2 RN's for the 70 patients. The nurses had Japanese helpers but I did not know to what level of nursing they were trained. In any case, these Japanese workers were great, but were very hard to understand when they spoke to me. I could see that some of these Marines had battle field colostomies and, compound fractures, severe burns, and what seemed to me to be, unfixable broken bodies. There was no way I was going to take the nurses away from these wounded young warriors. I did not feel worthy of receiving care while these young American Marines needed care. I wanted them to be seen first before any nurse could attend to me. So, when a wave of severe pain hit me, I covered my head under my pillow and silently cried, knowing that at least, the tears helped somewhat with the pain. Just to clarify, I was 25 years old and these young Marines considered me an "Old Man". Most if not all of these young Marines were between 18 to 19 years old.

Well, as I covered my head so no one could see my tears, I felt a soft hand touch on my leg and the person who touched me started talking to me. She said "I know you feel that you are not worthy of receiving pain medication because you see these Marines in pain and you prefer that we treat them first". "I want you to know that you are every bit as worthy and your pain is not any less then their pain". "I have time for them and I have time for you". "I have brought you the medication you need to help stop your pain". "I am going to give this medication to you now and I do not want to hear any arguments".

I took my pillow from my head and looked up to see this wonderful nurse who was the essence of love and devotion. I thanked her for her perception and kindness. She went on to give me an injection of Morphine which really helped my pain go away. There after, this same nurse made sure I received medication for pain throughout the day. This nurse even had time to say a small prayer with me when I asked her to pray with me. I truly believe that the Heavens heard my prayers and sent an Angel to respond to my medical needs as well as meeting the medical needs of these wounded young Marines and Sailors. When I was free of pain, I was able to help the nurses care for the Marines. The nurses taught me to do sterile procedures in caring for wounds. I was instructed on how to properly care for a colostomy. In short, since I was the only patient who could get up and move without help, my assignment was to do basic Nursing Care. I was also able to help these young Marines with their social and psychological issue relating to their "change in body image".

Because of my medical status, I was informed that I could no longer make the Navy my career. I was a career man and did not want to leave the Navy, but leave it I must. I asked what it would take to remain in the military service, and I was told that I would need to be a doctor, lawyer, or registered nurse. If I were to become any one of these, the military would take me back.

So, I had to start a new career. I began to think about that wonderful nurse who had such a positive attitude and gave her all to give the best care to her patients. If I could be just half as good of a nurse as she was, I was going to be a dynamite nurse. Well, that decided it for me. I was going to honor the memory of that nurse forever and I would choose Nursing as my new profession. After 40 years of nursing, I have retired. Still, I will never forget that period in my life where my prayers, a caring nurse, and the love of Jesus, spared this man pain, suffering, humiliation and allowed me to serve God just like all the other Angels we call Nurses.

Chapter seventeen - Pain from the sky:

As a teenager growing up in New York City, New York, I happened to live across the street from a large and very powerful Puerto Rican gang. Also, there were 4 other Puerto Rican gangs located in the near vicinity to my home. One of the tricks these gangs used to attack members of other gangs not in alliance with them is to go up on the roof tops of the apartment buildings and as the other gang members pass under their sights, the gang members would drop bricks, sticks, and all manner of debris on top of them.

One day as I got out of school I walked toward my house like I did every school day. As I walked home, a large rock hit my shoulder causing a great deal of pain. Before I knew it, I was being plummet by hundreds of rocks. Every time I tried to look up, I was hit on my face by what seemed a million smaller pieces of rocks. I was only one city block away from my house but I could see the rocks falling in front of me. I was scared beyond explanation. I felt that there must be thousands of gang members on the roof tops throwing down the rocks. I could not see any other gangs on the street, so I figured the gangs were after me. I tried zig zaging and going in circles, but no matter how hard I tried to escape, the rocks were still hitting me with precision and causing a great deal of pain. I began to pray asking Jesus to help me escape the gangs and the rocks they were throwing down upon me. I felt that their aim was excellent as I was being hit no matter what I did to avoid the rocks. As I prayed, my tears were flowing from my eyes and with my tears of fear and the tears of pain, I could hardly see where I was running. Some how, the rocks began to miss me and my vision cleared enough for me to see the stairway to my house. Although the rocks were still falling all around me, if I was hit, I did not feel the pain I previously felt prior to praying to Jesus. I finally made it up the stairs and into my house. I had lumps all over my head and so many bruises that my brothers and sisters could not count them all. I started crying again telling my family that at least 1 thousand gang members were up in the roof tops throwing rocks down on the people. My brother Juan laughed and told me that it was not rocks falling from the roof tops but hail. I thought I heard "hell" and agreed with my brother that it was truly hell. Again my brother laughed and corrected me by saying it was hail and spelled it out.

Never experiencing hail in my life, I did not believe him. My brother took me to the window and showed me the falling hail and that no gang members were on the roof. My brother was able to get a piece of hail and showed me that the hail is made of water that frozen before reaching the ground. Still, I knew that with the size of the hail and the quantity of hail balls that hit me, it was a miracle that all I had were lumps and bruises. I recalled praying to Jesus and feeling that from that moment on, if I was hit by the falling hail, I could no longer injured and the Heavens and Jesus allowed me to reach the safety of my home. As I looked from my window I could plainly see that anyone caught in the hail storm will surely die or be severely injured. I survived the equivalent of 500 yard of falling hail the size of golf balls to baseballs. I got down on my knees and profusely gave thanks to Lord Jesus for giving me a chance to continue living and continue to enjoy the blessings of His love. After that day I witness many hail storms. As I witness the hail storms, I remember the day that Jesus Love saved a scared and crying boy from certain injury or death.

CHAPTER EIGHTEEN - SWIM OR DROWN:

As a 9 year old I was envious of the other boys who could swim not only in the city's swimming pool, but also for being able to swim in the ocean. Although I could not swim, the boys who could swim allowed me to accompanied them to the East River in NYC and watch them swim. One of the boys, a boy who had my same first name of Carlos, was given the dare to swim under a barge and come out the other side. I looked at the barge and it looked like a giant beast to me. I asked Carlos not to take the dare, but since 5 other boys were also going to try it, Carlos agreed to go with them.

All six boys dived under the barge. Within a mere moment, the other five boys returned back to the starting point. They had set a trick just to get Carlos to try it. Unfortunately, as the boys climbed up the barge and went to the other side, Carlos did not appear. He had drowned and the current had carried his body several mile away where his body was found by some fishermen. Not knowing that Carlos had drowned, all the boys jumped into the river to try to find him. Forgetting that I could not swim, the boys pushed me into the river so I could help them find Carlos. I started to sink deeper into the river and I could feel the side of the barge near me. I did not want to drown but I did not know how to swim. I also did not know which side was up because the river water was dark with small oil slicks mixed with the river water. Yes, I panicked. I panicked but I did not forget to pray for forgiveness of my sins, although I don't recall having any sins at that time. As I prayed to Jesus and the Angels to save me, I started to float up towards the surface, Like any other object in the water, I too was carried away from my original place of entering the water. I finally reach the top of the water and took a breath before I went under again being taken further away yet still close to the side of the barge. I prayed again for help. I prayed what seemed to be an eternity. Please Jesus don't let me drown. As the current moved me along side of the barge, my hand grabbed a metal frame sticking out from the end of the barge. The frame turned out to be a ladder welded to the end of the barge that allowed crew members to board or depart from the barge. I hanged on for dear life. After resting a few moments, I grabbed the ladder with both hands and was able to raise my self out of the water. I stayed there for approximately 30 minutes until one of the boys noticed me and guided me up the stairs. I know that by all accounts, I also should have drowned that day. As I reached the top of the barge, I could see the other boys crying I was crying too, but my tears were tears thanking Jesus for giving me another chance at life. When I got home, I went to Carlos' mother and explain that her son tried to swim under a barge and did not reach the other side. Both myself and Carlos's mother prayed so that Carlos Soul would be at peace and in heaven with Jesus, God, and the Angels. When I told her that I almost drowned by the same barge, she told me that it was Jesus love that did not want another mother to suffer the loss of a child. I sincerely believe that my prayers and Jesus love saved me that day.

Chapter nineteen - Crossing the flood:

I had just departed my family in Florida and was on my way home to California. While in Florida, I introduce my children to my father, their grandfather. I had a marvelous time with my father and my brothers and sisters. With only 4 days left in my leave, I said my goodbyes and loaded up my car and began my trip back to California where I lived and where my duty station is located. The trip across America was going well and if all went well, I would arrive in California with one day to spare. Like many military men, I was in no hurry to return to duty any earlier than I need. I knew that the trip across America will take me three days of driving. So with four days left on my leave, I felt I had plenty of time to drive across America and rest one day before I reported back to duty. All was going well until I reach the State of Texas. It felt like driving through Texas was taking 4 days by itself. After driving in Texas for 10 hours, a rain storm hit the area I was driving in. The rain storm was so severe that the Texas Highway Patrol stopped all traffic until it was safe to drive the highway again. To my dismay, the rain storm lasted till the next morning. What almost stop my heart was that the rain fall had flooded the roads as well as the land for miles on each side of the highway. I knew that I had to return to my duty station or face being AWOL (Absent without Leave). The Highway Patrol car was parked on the side of the road with its light flashing advising motorist that if they crossed into the flooded road, it will be at their risk. I could see at least 20 abandoned cars that their drivers had attempted to drive pass the patrol car and into the flooded road. I had no choice. Either I attempted to drive on the flooded road or be classified as AWOL. I explained to the Texas Patrolman that I had no other choice. He understood but pointed to the cars who attempted to drive in the flooded road and had failed.

Asking God and Jesus for guidance I notice that on both sides of the road were telephone poles and highway signs. I believed the only reason I was able to think about these poles and highway signs was because the good Lord Jesus wanted me to see that if I drove in the middle of the road and stayed in-between the poles and signs, I would be able to drive on the shallow part of the flooded road and reach the end of the 20 miles of flooded roads. I explained my plan to the Patrolman and I again said my prayers for safety for my family and for anyone who followed me into the flooded road. When I looked back in my rearview mirror, the Patrolman and at least 15 other cars lined up behind me. With my belief that Jesus was not going to abandoned me, I drove into the flooded road driving in the middle and since the road was not visible, I stayed in-between the telephone poles and highway signs.

I was so focus on following the instructions I believed came from heaven that I did not realized that I had drove pass the flooded road and onto the other side where the road was free of flood. The Patrolman passed me up and beeped his horn. Soon, most of the cars trailing behind me passed me up and each greeted me with a honk of their horn. I gave thanks to God and to Jesus for guiding me through a flood that had stopped many drivers. I made it home safe and reported to my duty on time. I will never forget the flood and I certainly will never forget that it was Jesus Love that allowed me to reach the other side safely.

Chapter twenty - The Republican River and lightning:

At age 14 I was living with my family at Fort Riley, Kansas. My father was stationed their while serving in the U.S. Army. Kansas was a new and interesting world to me. Growing up in NYC did not allow me to experience the wonders of the outdoors and wide open spaces. Fort Riley became a giant play ground to me and my brothers and sisters. In my first summer in Kansas, my nephew came to spend the summer with us. My nephew was 13 and seemed more wiser in the way of the world than I was. One day, two twin brothers that lived two houses from us invited my nephew to join them on a raft ride down the Republican River. My nephew invited me and since I never been on a raft, I wanted dearly to go. When I asked my father, he did not give me permission saying that the Republican River can be dangerous, especially for boys who do not know their way in river safety. I was disappointed and told the twins and my nephew that I could not go with them. When my father left for work, my nephew convinced me that we were going to return by 3 p.m., two hours before my dad would return from work. Wanting to badly to go, I disobeyed my father's restriction and joined the twins and my nephew at the launching ramp. The raft consisted of 4 large metal barrels with a wood deck. I helped the boys push the raft into the river and jumped on the wooden deck. The river was flowing quite rapidly but none of us notice the speed. We were just having the time of our lives. Without noticing the change in weather, we continued to enjoy or ride. Soon it began to rain. Within 15 minutes, the wind picked up and lighting flashed in the dark sky.

I wanted to stop the raft and get out of the river. One of the twin brothers felt like I did and starting yelling at his brother to stop the raft. Soon the two brothers began to fight on the raft. All of us were almost thrown overboard by their fighting and shaking the raft. My nephew and I were able to stop the twins from continuing the fight.

It became very clear to all of us that we were in deep trouble. Just as we felt the fear of the danger we were in, lightning began to fall in the river in front of us. We definitely panicked. We tried to paddle the raft to the shore but the force of the river was greater than the strength we had to paddle against it. With the twins and my nephew yelling for help, I decided that I needed to ask for forgiveness for disobeying my father and for getting into this dangerous situation. I ignored the yelling of the others and began to pray. I knew without doubt that I was going to die and that the others on the raft were going to die too. I asked Jesus to pray for us and for our families. I prayed to Jesus that if it was at all possible, that He find a way to save us from this ride of death. The lightning stilled continued to fall a hundred yards in front of the moving raft.

I was able to calm the other boys down enough to get them to work together and try again to guide the raft toward the banks of the river. I prayed and prayed. "Dear Jesus, please save us".

All of a sudden, a swell pushed the raft towards the bank of the river and the raft caught tree roots that were close to the shore. The raft held it place inter twined by the tree roots. Seeing a chance to save ourselves, I told the others to follow me and jump into the river and swim to the river bank. At first they hesitated and watched me trying to make it to shore. When the raft started to move again, all three boys jumped into the water and with God's help, we all made it to the banks. The problem now was to be able to climb the slope of the river bands that had become muddy and slippery by the rain. Again I prayed. Help us dear Jesus, help us get to the top of these slopes. After many attempts, all of us made it to the top of the river banks and noticed the highway was just 10 yards away from us. I thank God and I thank Jesus for the help they provided us. I strongly believed that without Jesus intervention, all of us would have drowned. Still, we were not out of trouble yet. It was raining, we were soaked to the bone, and our clothes were muddy. As prayed to thank Lord Jesus, I asked Jesus if he could guide us to get home safely. I did not realize that the river had taken us close to 200 miles away from where we started.

As the four of us walked, I continued to pray. Praying to thank the Lord for saving us many times and praying that he continued to stay with us until we made it safely back home. After walking 20 minutes, a man drove passed us and suddenly he stopped. Each of us ran to his car. When I reached the car I asked the man if he could help us by notifying our parents in Fort Riley that we need them to pick us up. The man looked at our dirty and muddy clothes and asked us to get inside the car that he would take us to our parents. His car had been clean and shinny. Yet he did not hesitate to let us get in his car. He was the one to inform us that we were close to 200 miles away from Fort Riley. The driver made one stop to phone our parents to inform them that we were safe and that he would bring us home. During the trip home, I thanked this man for his kindness to strangers and for allowing us shelter, even if it meant that his clean car would take several cleanings before it would look clean again. He accepted my thanks and told me to think nothing of it. On the way home I thanked Jesus for having wonderful people like this man on Earth. I continued to pray for forgiveness for my disobedience. When we finally arrived at home, I expected my father to give me a scolding and a whipping with his belt. I got neither. Instead, I was given a hug and stated that he was happy that we made it safe. He did tell me to learn a lesson from this and never disobey him again. Believe me, I never did. That night I thank Jesus and God for giving me such understanding parents.

CHAPTER TWENTY-ONE - PRAYING
FOR THE WELFARE OF OTHERS:

Most of the encounters where our good Lord Jesus intervene in my behalf was preceded by my intense prayers seeking Lord Jesus' help. I will like to share with you an incident that showed me that Lord Jesus also helps those we pray for.

In 1966 I was stationed in Rota, Spain, a U.S. Naval base in the southern part of Spain approximately 2 hours from the city of Cadiz and close to 11/2 hours from Seville, Spain. As a high ranking Petty Officer, my salary was about 700 dollars a month.

When the $700 dollars was changed into Spanish money, the amount of my paycheck was about 4,500 Pesetas, or the money system of Spain. The local people did not make no where that sum of money, so to them, I was a rich person. I lived in a medium size chalet that had 4 bedrooms, a kitchen, living room, and a very spacious back yard full of chickens and rabbits. I purchased most of my food inside the Base at the Commissary. The food quality was excellent and our meals were satisfying and nutritional. One day I got off work every early and as I drove down the road that led to my chalet, I noticed 5 children looking into the trash bins that I filled with my trash and food that was not eaten. As I watched the children, I saw them sharing the discarded food among themselves. The horror of seeing children eating out of a garbage can almost cause me to pass out or have a heart attack. I pulled my car over and approached the children. At first they were terrified of my presence. They knew that this trash bin belonged to me. I approached them softly and asked them if they were hungry. At first, no one replied. I asked again adding that I was not upset or angry and that I just wanted to help them. Finally, the oldest of the children, a 9 year old girl, told me that yes they are hungry and that yes, they come here everyday to find food to eat. It was one of those moments that make you feel sick in your stomach yet feel very sorry for these children while thanking

God that you yourself do not have to experience this type of hunger. I gained their trust and they escorted me to the place they were living in. When I walked in the house, a lady with a weak and sick sounding voice asked me who I was and what did I want from her. I told her that I was one of her neighbors and if she will allow me to help all of them, I would be happy to do so. The children's mother informed me that her husband had died two years before and in the past 3 months, she had become too ill to work or to take proper care of their children. I informed her that I could get a doctor to see her and that I could pay for her medications and for the doctor visits.

She wanted to say no, but in her heart I believe she felt my sincerity and my true desire to help her and her children. First, I went home and got potato and steaks that I had plan to eat that evening. I added vegetables and desert. I cooked the meal in my kitchen and brought the food to them at their home. The children told me that it had been a long time since they had eaten a complete meal. When they were not able to beg for food, they would raid my trash bin, witch seem to be daily. I got several of my sailor companions and explained the situation. My married friends volunteered their wives to wash the children's clothes and I hired a woman to clean the house and return every two days to maintain the house cleanliness. I purchased a refrigerator with an electricity sensing motor to keep the fluctuating electricity from burning up the refrigerator. Because I was Spanish and English speaking, I held nightly classed to teach English to the Spanish and teach Spanish to the Americans. With this extra money, I purchased enough food so that the children did not have to eat from garbage cans while I lived there. The one thing that I could not fix was the mother's health. She had been sick too long and the doctors felt that she may die at any moment. I got down on my knees and began to pray that Lord Jesus, God Almighty, and every Archangel in heaven help this lady get better. I find that throughout my life I have asked the Lord Jesus to help me with situations beyond my control, but this situation required more prayers than I could ever pray. I cover the cost of doctors coming in every day and I cover the cost of medication with no thought of repayment or for any gratitude from the family. I did what I could because it was the right thing to do and God had given me the financial means to provide help in His name. After 4 days of daily medical visits and eating a proper diet, the mother began to show signs of improving.

I did not let up on my prayers. In two weeks the mother was able to take care of herself and her children. She just needed a job so that she could provide food for their children. Again I prayed for assistance in finding a suitable job that was within this lady's capabilities. Two days later I was able to find a job for her that allowed her to enter the base and take care of 2 children and maintain the home. This job gave her a decent salary that she was able to change into Spanish money and provide for her children. I continued to help the family for three more years. When I departed from Spain, the lady had remarried and the children were going to school. More than anything else, the children were happy and healthy. I thanked Lord Jesus for allowing me to help this family and for hearing my prayers for heavenly help for that family.

CHAPTER TWENTY-TWO - FEAR AND THE DEVIL:

While I was writing my first book, Mallory of the Angels - Conquest of Hell, I felt what appeared to be dark, sharp daggers being pointed at me. I was writing a book in which God got fed up with the evil on earth and the evils caused by Lucifer in Hell. God decided in my book to destroy all evil in Hell and on Earth. Any evil entity wanting forgiveness would receive forgiveness, those that refused forgiveness, would be destroyed. God also offered this deal to Lucifer. After the beginning chapters, I got specific on how evil was going to be destroyed on earth. I felt an evil presence that tried to scare me from continuing the book. It could have been in my imagination, but I don't believe so. I felt these evil presences were telling me that I could suffer deadly consequences if I continued writing the book. The threat of harm was also extended to my family. In fact, I believe I received so many evil threats that I could count on an attack for every chapter I wrote.

With each chapter I wrote, I got the feeling that an unknown evil power was trying to interfere and either delay or prevent me from completing my story.

I did, however, have my back covered. Before I wrote the book, I prayed to the Lord Jesus and God for guidance and for protection against evil. The reply I received was to proceed with the book "full speed ahead" and to "fear no evil". I was reminded that whenever I am surrounded by evil darkness, all I have to do is to light the light of the Lord Jesus and God in my heart and in my mind and no evil would dare approach me. So that is exactly what I did.

I feel that I am blessed. In fact, I feel that throughout each section of my life, the Lord Jesus not only walked by my side, but also walked the so called "mile" in my shoes.

Thank you for allowing me to share these few moments when Jesus walked a mile in my shoes.

THE END.